DANNY AND THE DEEP BLUE SEA

AN APACHE DANCE
BY JOHN PATRICK SHANLEY

DANNY AND THE DEEP BLUE SEA was presented at the Circle in the Square Theatre, in New York City, June 6, 1984. It was directed by Barnet Kellman; the scenery was designed by David Gropman; the lighting was designed by Richard Nelson; and the costumes were designed by Marcia Dixcy. The cast was as follows:

ROBERTA .... June Stein
DANNY .... John Turturro

DANNY AND THE DEEP BLUE SEA received its professional premiere at Actors Theatre of Louisville in February, 1984.

DANNY AND THE DEEP BLUE SEA was originally presented as a staged reading at the 1983 National Playwrights Conference at the Eugene O'Neill Memorial Theater Center.

NOTE: All groups licensed to present DANNY AND THE DEEP BLUE SEA are required to include the credits listed above in all programs and advertising issued in connection with their productions.

This play is dedicated to everyone in the Bronx who punched me or kissed me, and to everyone whom I punched or kissed.

CHARACTERS

ROBERTA: 31 years old. Blue jeans, a cheap dress-up blouse that's gotten ratty. She's physically depleted, with nervous bright eyes.
DANNY: 29 years old. Chinos and pullover shirt. He's dark and powerful. He finds it difficult to meet Roberta's gaze.
About Both Characters: They are violent and battered, inarticulate and yearning to speak, dangerous and vulnerable.

A DEFINITION

An Apache Dance is a violent dance for two people, originated by the Parisian apaches. Parisian apaches are gangsters or ruffians.

STYLE

This play is emotionally real, but does not take place in a realistic world. Only those scenic elements necessary to the action should be on stage. Only those areas that are played in should be lit.

DANNY AND THE DEEP BLUE SEA

*Two tables, each illuminated by its own shaded light. Roberta
sits at one in a vacant sulk, nursing a beer and picking at a bowl
of pretzels. Enter Danny, with a pitcher of beer and a glass. He
sits at the other. His hands are badly bruised, and one of his
cheeks is cut. He pours himself a beer. A moment passes.*

DANNY. How 'bout a pretzel?
ROBERTA. No. They're mine.
DANNY. You ain't gonna eat all of 'em. Lemme have one.
ROBERTA. Fuck off.
DANNY. All right.
ROBERTA. You wanna pretzel?
DANNY. Yeah. (*Roberta picks up the bowl, takes it to Danny's table,
and goes straight back to her seat.*)
ROBERTA. You can have 'em. I'm finished with 'em.
DANNY. Thanks.
ROBERTA. You're welcome.
DANNY. You want some of my beer?
ROBERTA. No.
DANNY. Some fuckin bar. Nobody here.
ROBERTA. That's why I like it.
DANNY. What's the matter? You don't like people?
ROBERTA. No. Not really.
DANNY. Me neither.
ROBERTA. What happened to your hands?
DANNY. Fight.
ROBERTA. Who'd you fight?
DANNY. I don't know. Some guys last night. Tonight too.
ROBERTA. Two fights?
DANNY. Yeah.
ROBERTA. How come?

DANNY. I don't know. Guys bother me, I start swinging.
ROBERTA. I don't get it. Did they say something to you?
DANNY. (*Exploding.*) Who the fuck asked you to get it! Ain't none a your fuckin business I lock horns with anybody! Nobody crosses my fuckin line, man! They can do what they want out there, but nobody crosses my fuckin line!
ROBERTA. All right.
DANNY. They asked me where I was going.
ROBERTA. Who?
DANNY. The guys I was fighting tonight.
ROBERTA. They asked where you were going.
DANNY. That's right. So I decked the first guy. Hit him in the nose. You hit 'em in the nose, they can't see.
ROBERTA. Why not?
DANNY. I don't know. But it's true.
ROBERTA. All right.
DANNY. But while I was hittin on him, the other guy got me with his belt.
ROBERTA. That musta hurt.
DANNY. Yeah. I made him eat that fuckin belt!
ROBERTA. Where you from?
DANNY. Zerega.
ROBERTA. Yeah? I used to catch frogs from over at Zerega.
DANNY. Ain't no frogs 'round Zerega.
ROBERTA. Not now. When I was a kid.
DANNY. Ain't never been no frogs 'round Zerega.
ROBERTA. Yes, there was. There used to be a little like marsh over on Zerega, and it had frogs in it.
DANNY. When?
ROBERTA. A long time ago.
DANNY. How old's that make you?
ROBERTA. Thirty-one.
DANNY. I'm twenty-nine. When I turn thirty I'm gonna put a gun in my mouth and blow my fuckin head off.
ROBERTA. Do it in the bathroom. It's easier to clean up.
DANNY. I'm gonna do it!
ROBERTA. Why you say a thing like that?
DANNY. I don't know.
ROBERTA. Ain't no different to be thirty.
DANNY. It's gotta be different.

ROBERTA. I'm thirty-one.
DANNY. I heard ya. That's you! Me, I'm twenty-nine and I can't stay the way I am for too fuckin long.
ROBERTA. Why not?
DANNY. Cause I can't!
ROBERTA. You from Zerega whaddaya doing here?
DANNY. There's nothing goin on over Zerega.
ROBERTA. Nothing going on here.
DANNY. Yeah, well maybe I like that. Peaceful.
ROBERTA. You don't look peaceful to me.
DANNY. I'm peaceful. But people fuck with me.
ROBERTA. Why don't you come over, sit with me.
DANNY. I don't wanna. This is good where I am.
ROBERTA. All right.
DANNY. I'm sorry.
ROBERTA. That's all right.
DANNY. Is that guy looking at me?
ROBERTA. Who? Fred? No, he's sleeping. He's drunk. Can't you see, his mouth's open.
DANNY. Oh, yeah. There's light on his glasses. I couldn't see his eyes. I thought he was looking at me.
ROBERTA. What if he was?
DANNY. I'd beat his fuckin face in. (*They both laugh.*)
DANNY. You from here?
ROBERTA. Yeah.
DANNY. Where?
ROBERTA. Right up the block.
DANNY. What, you married?
ROBERTA. Divorced.
DANNY. Gotta kid?
ROBERTA. Yeah.
DANNY. Who's takin care of the kid?
ROBERTA. My mother. My mother always takes care of the kid.
DANNY. That's a good deal.
ROBERTA. Yeah. You gotta friend, you know, a girlfriend?
DANNY. No.
ROBERTA. No?
DANNY. We broke up.
ROBERTA. What was her name?

DANNY. Cecilia.
ROBERTA. Italian?
DANNY. Yeah.
ROBERTA. I'm Italian.
DANNY. She gave me a pain in my ass! She was very fine, but she'd make me go to her house. Sit around with her fuckin parents. And she'd talk in this totally fuckin phoney-ass way when her parents were around. Would you like a glass of soda, Danny? Oh, please be careful with your cigarette, Danny. Like she wasn't the same one I humped inna pay toilet! I'm sorry. I gotta bad mouth.
ROBERTA. Maybe she had to play phoney cause her parents were drivin her crazy?
DANNY. I don't think so.
ROBERTA. I hate my father. If I thought I wouldn't get in bad trouble I'd take a big knife and stab him in the face about fifty times.
DANNY. I hate my father, too.
ROBERTA. Yeah?
DANNY. He's dead, but I hate him anyway. He was a meat-packer. He used to get real mad all the time. One time he got so mad cause somebody did something, that he just fuckin died.
ROBERTA. I wish my father would die. He was the one who made me get married. This guy I knew got me pregnant. I was like eighteen. And my father made me get married to him. He wasn't a bad guy. We moved into this apartment. I was scared. But it was nice, too. I started, you know, to decorate. And then my parents started comin over all the time. This is how you put up curtains. This is how you wash the floor. My fuckin mother started cookin the fuckin meals! And this guy, my husband, he was like, What the fuck is goin on? His parents were cool. Just like called once in a while on the phone. I felt so bad. Sick in the morning. Mother knockin on the door by twelve o'clock. My father comin in after work. And the guy, my husband, when he got there. It was like, Who the fuck are you?
DANNY. What's your name?
ROBERTA. Roberta.
DANNY. Mine's Danny.
ROBERTA. Sometimes I just start screaming, you know? For no reason at all. My mother thinks I'm crazy. Maybe you're

right. Maybe I shoulda shot myself in the head when I turned thirty.
DANNY. You want some beer?
ROBERTA. Sure. (*Danny brings over pitcher, pours some beer, and then goes back to his table.*)
ROBERTA. You waitin for somebody?
DANNY. No.
ROBERTA. Me neither.
DANNY. I don't know anybody anymore.
ROBERTA. I got a girlfriend. Shirley. She lives next door to me. Always has. Never got married. We used to have good times when we were kids. We both had long hair and we'd go bicycle riding. I have a picture home. We looked great. She's a pig now. She goes to these bars up in the two hundreds. They got live bands. Guys pick her up. She goes in cars with 'em. She'll get in any guy's car. We used to sniff glue in my bedroom and get fucked up. She uses a lotta dope now. I use some, but she uses a lot.
DANNY. I think I killed a guy last night.
ROBERTA. How?
DANNY. I beat him up.
ROBERTA. Well, that's not killing a guy.
DANNY. I don't know.
ROBERTA. What happened?
DANNY. I was at this party. A guy named Skull. Everybody was getting fucked up. Somebody said there was some guys outside. I went out. There were these two guys from another neighborhood out there. I asked 'em what they were doing there. They knew somebody. One of 'em was a big guy. Real drunk. He said they wanted to go, but something about twenty dollars. I told him to give me the twenty dollars, but he didn't have it. I started hitting him. But when I hit him, it never seemed to be hard, you know? I hit him a lot in the chest and face but it didn't seem to do nothing. I had him over a car hood. His friend wanted to take him away. I said okay. They started to go down the block. And they started to fight. So I ran after them. I hit on the little guy a minute, and then I started working on the big guy again. Everybody just watched. I hit him as hard as I could for about ten minutes. It never seemed like enough. Then I looked at his face . . . His teeth were all broken. He fell down.

I stomped on his fuckin chest and I heard something break. I grabbed him under the arms and pushed him over a little fence. Into somebody's driveway. Somebody pointed to some guy and said he had the twenty dollars. I kicked him in the nuts. He went right off the ground. Then I left.

ROBERTA. You probably didn't kill him.

DANNY. I don't know.

ROBERTA. I seen a lotta people get beat up. They looked real bad, but they were all right.

DANNY. It don't matter.

ROBERTA. You ever been in jail?

DANNY. No.

ROBERTA. I wonder what it's like. Maybe it's crazy, but sometimes I think I'd like it.

DANNY. Why?

ROBERTA. I don't know. Just a change of scenery to keep me from going off my nut.

DANNY. I don't get it.

ROBERTA. What?

DANNY. You don't make me mad.

ROBERTA. So?

DANNY. Everybody makes me mad. That's why I don't ever talk to nobody. That's why I'm sittin in this fuckin bar. I don't feel like walkin home. I feel like I'm gonna have to fight everybody in the whole fuckin Bronx to get home. And I'm too tired to fight everybody.

ROBERTA. You live with your mother?

DANNY. Yeah.

ROBERTA. Think she's worried?

DANNY. My mother's a fuckin dishrag. Dishrag's don't worry.

ROBERTA. Is she stupid?

DANNY. I don't know.

ROBERTA. Well, what's she like?

DANNY. She works in a bakery. She gotta get up real early. When she comes home, she throws up.

ROBERTA. Why?

DANNY. From the sweetness. The smell of the sweetness is too much, and it makes her puke.

ROBERTA. My mother's nervous. There's something wrong with her thyroid.

DANNY. Why don't you rip her fuckin thyroid out?
ROBERTA. I don't know. (*Roberta comes over and joins Danny at his table.*)
DANNY. What are you doin?
ROBERTA. I'm lonely.
DANNY. I think you're makin me mad.
ROBERTA. Cause I'm sittin here?
DANNY. Cause you want something, and I am definitely not up to fuckin nothin! You don't understand! I'm jumpin out of my fuckin skin! Everything hurts! I could bite your fuckin head! Leave me alone! Everything hurts! (*She grabs him by the shirt.*)
ROBERTA. You're crazy, you know that?
DANNY. Yeah, I know.
ROBERTA. You're lucky you don't stutter. You're lucky you don't bite your fuckin tongue! You're a lucky guy!
DANNY. What the fuck you sayin?
ROBERTA. Nothing you could understand, alright?
DANNY. You calling me stupid?
ROBERTA. I'm calling you crazy, Crazy! But what you don't know is I'm crazy, too! Yeah. You don't know me! I could do anything. I did something so awful. I ain't even gonna tell you what. If I told you, you wouldn't even look at me. (*She lets go of his shirt.*)
DANNY. There ain't nothing you coulda done would seem like anything to me. What'd you do?
ROBERTA. I'm not gonna tell you.
DANNY. Look, I think I killed a guy. What could be worse than that?
ROBERTA. Suckin off your father.
DANNY. What?
ROBERTA. A daughter suckin off her father. That'd be worse than killin somebody, wouldn't it?
DANNY. Did you do that?
ROBERTA. Answer me!
DANNY. I don't know. No. Did you do that?
ROBERTA. Yeah.
DANNY. I thought you hated the guy?
ROBERTA. Yeah, I always did. I always hated him and wanted to run away. But then, after, I hated him different. So I

wanted to stick a butcher knife in his nose. Ja! Right in the middle of his nose. And then pull down slow till I got to his mouth.
DANNY. That wouldn't kill him. I don't think it would.
ROBERTA. It'd be good. People'd ask him why I did it, and he'd say, I don't know. But he'd know.
DANNY. I'm havin trouble breathin.
ROBERTA. Why? What's wrong?
DANNY. I start thinkin about it. Whenever I start thinkin about breathin, I can't breathe right.
ROBERTA. So forget it.
DANNY. A guy told me, if you think you're gonna have a heart attack, if you keep thinkin about it, even if your heart was alright to begin with, in the end, you'll have one. You can make your heart go bad.
ROBERTA. That's bullshit.
DANNY. It's true!
ROBERTA. How do you know?
DANNY. I can feel it happening! I don't wanna die like that. I don't wanna die from my own mind. I gotta think about something else. Davy Crockett. (*Sings.*) Davy! Davy Crockett. . . !
ROBERTA. He came into my room. He was drunk. It was real real dark. He was mad cause I'd gone out partyin and my mother was away and nobody'd been watching the kid. He was yellin at me and I was thinkin, He yells and I do nothin. So I started cryin and sayin I was sorry. He put his hand on my face. I put my hand out and I touched him. There. He got quiet. That's what did it. I made him get quiet. I could never make him do anything. That's why I did it. So I could make him do things. That was the only time. There was one other time after that when he wanted me to, but I wouldn't. And that was good, too. Right then.
DANNY. I was supposed to marry this girl Cecilia. I called her Sissy. She liked that, but she wouldn't let me call her that in front of her parents. I don't know what was with her and her parents.
ROBERTA. Did you hear what I told you about me and my father?
DANNY. Yeah, I heard.
ROBERTA. Would you be able to kiss a girl who'd done that?

DANNY. It don't mean nothin to me.
ROBERTA. Really?
DANNY. Sure really.
ROBERTA. Would you kiss me?
DANNY. What, you don't get kissed?
ROBERTA. Nobody knows but you.
DANNY. What'd you tell me for?
ROBERTA. I don't know.
DANNY. Well, I won't tell nobody.
ROBERTA. That don't help.
DANNY. What d'you want?
ROBERTA. How am I gonna get rid of this!
DANNY. What?
ROBERTA. What I done!
DANNY. I don't know.
ROBERTA. I can't stay like I am! I can't stay in this fuckin head anymore! If I don't get outta this fuckin head I'm gonna go crazy! I could eat glass! I could put my hand inna fire an watch the fuckin thing burn and I still wouldn't be outta this fuckin head! What am I gonna do? What? I can't close my eyes, man. I can't close my eyes and see the things I see. I'm still in that house! I wouldn't a believed it but I'm still in that house. He's there and I'm there. And my kid. Who's nuts already. It's like, what could happen now? You know? What else could happen? But somethin's gotta. I feel like the day's gonna come when I could just put out my arm and fire and lightning will come outta my hand and burn up everything for a thousand miles! It ain't right to feel as much as I feel.
DANNY. What you tellin me for?
ROBERTA. No reason, all right?
DANNY. You want something.
ROBERTA. So what. Don't you?
DANNY. No.
ROBERTA. Liar.
DANNY. Hey, you wanna smack? I don't lie!
ROBERTA. So what if you did, it ain't so terrible.
DANNY. I don't lie!
ROBERTA. All right.
DANNY. I'm tellin you the truth. I don't want nothin from you.

ROBERTA. I got a good deal in my house. I got somethin it's almost like my own apartment. When you get to the top of the stairs, there's a separate door to the room I sleep in. Don't have to deal with my parents at all if I go right in that room. I'd never deal with 'em if it weren't for the kid.
DANNY. I'm not goin anywhere with you.
ROBERTA. Who asked you to? So what are you goin to do?
DANNY. Stay here, drink my beer.
ROBERTA. All night?
DANNY. That's right.
ROBERTA. The place closes.
DANNY. So when it closes, I'll go someplace else!
ROBERTA. All the places close.
DANNY. I'll go someplace else!
ROBERTA. And get in a fight, right?
DANNY. Maybe. If people fuck with me!
ROBERTA. Ain't no maybe. You're gonna haveta fight. Because you were right. You're gonna haveta fight every motherfuckin body in the Bronx. And even it probably won't get you home.
DANNY. You don't know.
ROBERTA. I know.
DANNY. Get off my case, bitch!
ROBERTA. Come home with me.
DANNY. What for?
ROBERTA. Cause you're the one I told.
DANNY. That ain't no reason.
ROBERTA. Oh, yes it is! It is to me.
DANNY. No.
ROBERTA. Let me ask you something.
DANNY. I ain't tellin you shit.
ROBERTA. Tell me why your hands are all ripped up.
DANNY. I got in a fight!
ROBERTA. And that mark on your face.
DANNY. I got in a fight, I told ya!
ROBERTA. Yeah, you told me.
DANNY. That's right.
ROBERTA. And you think you killed somebody.
DANNY. That's right, too.
ROBERTA. Why?

DANNY. Shut up!

ROBERTA. I wanna know.

DANNY. What are you, a fuckin social worker! Shut up I said!

ROBERTA. Why don't you tell me before somethin happens and you can't tell me no more?

DANNY. You're tryin ta cross my fuckin line, man!

ROBERTA. That's right! I am. I've been sittin here starin at a spot on the wall for about a thousand years, and if I don't talk to somebody about somethin, somethin that means somethin, I'm gonna snap out! You understand? I'm gonna snap the fuck out!

DANNY. Don't you work no shit on my head or I'll kill ya, understand?

ROBERTA. I understand, okay? I just don't give a flyin fuck.

DANNY. You can do what you want out there, but don't you cross my line or you'll be dead!

ROBERTA. Then I'll be dead. That scares me about as much as Halloween.

DANNY. Don't push me.

ROBERTA. Why not? What else I got to do to pass the fuckin time!

DANNY. Don't, I'm tellin ya!

ROBERTA. I know, I know. You're a cold killer with a hair trigger and I better tiptoe outta your way before I get wasted. Pardon me if I don't faint.

DANNY. Please!

ROBERTA. You don't scare me, asshole. I see worse than you crawlin around in my sink. You're about as bad as a faggot in his Sunday dress! Your mama probably still gives you her tit when you get shook up! (*She starts slapping him.*) What's the matter, badass? Somebody get your matches wet? This your time of the month? Huh? Huh? You don't remember how to pop your fuckin cork? Huh? Or do you get off on pigs rubbin their shoes on your ugly dick-lick face, you lowlife beefcake faggot! (*Snapping out, he roars and chokes her. She doesn't struggle.*)

DANNY. I told you! I told you!

ROBERTA. I . . . got . . .

DANNY. You can't push me!

ROBERTA. Harder.

DANNY. (*Lets her go in horror.*) Jesus!

ROBERTA. Why'd you stop?

DANNY. Don't talk to me.
ROBERTA. Who am I gonna talk to if I don't talk to you?
DANNY. (*Starts to cry.*) Leave me alone.
ROBERTA. No.
DANNY. Everybody leave me alone.
ROBERTA. Why you so quick with your hands?
DANNY. I don't know.
ROBERTA. You know.
DANNY. I'm too full.
ROBERTA. What?
DANNY. I'm too full . . . for anything . . . to move right. I can't . . . Watch out.
ROBERTA. Talk.
DANNY. Watch out. Listen. I can't stop myself if I hit you.
ROBERTA. That's all right. I don't care and I'm not scared.
DANNY. People can't talk to me anymore.
ROBERTA. I hear you.
DANNY. I can't work anymore. They don't want me on the truck.
ROBERTA. I hear you.
DANNY. It's like they don't listen to what they say to each other. If they was listenin, they'd have to start swingin. They'd have to.
ROBERTA. But you listen.
DANNY. I don't want to.
ROBERTA. But it ain't a question a want.
DANNY. No.
ROBERTA. It's how you are.
DANNY. They talk to each other. Nobody talks to me. I'm alone wherever I am.
ROBERTA. Me too.
DANNY. I start to think, I'm breathin, I'm breathin, and then that gets hard to do cause I'm thinkin about it, and I start to think about gettin a heart attack, and I feel pain, O NO, everything hurts! Everything hurts! Why does it keep on when I can't do anything. Somebody help me!
ROBERTA. I'll help you.
DANNY. Somebody help me.
ROBERTA. I'll help you, baby.
DANNY. Everything hurts all the time.

ROBERTA. I know, I know.

DANNY. The only thing that stops it is when I hit on somebody. Then I'm nobody and it's just the other guy I see. I can just jump on him and outta me. Make it go out, out!

ROBERTA. I'm gonna take you home, baby.

DANNY. I don't wanna.

ROBERTA. Yes, you do.

DANNY. What for?

ROBERTA. For love.

DANNY. Love?

ROBERTA. We're gonna love each other.

DANNY. I can't do that.

ROBERTA. We're gonna love each other. I hear the birds in the morning at my window. It always hurts me. We'll hear the birds in the morning.

DANNY. I gotta go home.

ROBERTA. You got no home.

DANNY. Yes, I do.

ROBERTA. You got no home. Just like me.

DANNY. I gotta go home.

ROBERTA. My poor sweetheart. He's gotta go home but he's got no home.

DANNY. No. You're right. I don't.

ROBERTA. Me neither. I got no home neither. But I'm gonna take you home, baby, and it's gonna be there.

DANNY. The guys I work with. The guys on the truck. They call me the Beast.

ROBERTA. No.

DANNY. They call me the Beast.

ROBERTA. Come on. Let's get outta here. Let's go home. (*They exit, slowly and quietly. The lights go down.*)

SCENE 2

Roberta and Danny on a mattress on the floor of a little room with no right angles. Somewhere above them is a small, crooked window. The colors of the room are slate blues and dove grays. A little lamp sits D.R., on a little stool; it's lit. There's some shelv-

19

ing, left. A doll, dressed as a bride, stands on one of the shelves.
They've just finished.

ROBERTA. So what's your name?
DANNY. Danny. What, you forget already?
ROBERTA. No, I remember now.
DANNY. Yours is Roberta.
ROBERTA. You got a good memory.
DANNY. No big deal.
ROBERTA. You didn't mind?
DANNY. What?
ROBERTA. Doin it with me?
DANNY. No.
ROBERTA. After what I told you? About my father?
DANNY. No. Why would I care?
ROBERTA. Don't be stupid. You want somethin to drink?
DANNY. Whaddaya got?
ROBERTA. I got some red wine.
DANNY. Okay. (*She gets up, goes to a little shelf, pulls out a bottle of
wine and a metal cup.*)
ROBERTA. I only got the one cup.
DANNY. That's okay. I'll drink outta the bottle.
ROBERTA. No. Would you mind? We could both drink from
the one cup.
DANNY. No, I don't mind. (*She pours, sips, and passes the cup to
him. She watches him a moment, till he drinks.*) It tastes like piss.
ROBERTA. I'll light a candle.
DANNY. All right.
ROBERTA. You like my room?
DANNY. Yeah. It's good.
ROBERTA. It used to be a closet. I painted it myself.
DANNY. Uh-huh.
ROBERTA. I light this candle and I close this door . . . You
see that round light up on that roof?
DANNY. Yeah, I see it.
ROBERTA. The guy who lives over there put that light up
because he's got a pigeon coop, and people were stealin his
pigeons. Don't you think it looks like the moon?
DANNY. No.
ROBERTA. Come on, look at it!

DANNY. All right. Yeah, it does a little.
ROBERTA. Like a full moon every night. (*Danny howls.*)
ROBERTA. Shut up! What are you doin?
DANNY. Howlin at the moon.
ROBERTA. Oh. Well, you ain't no wolf out in the woods, so keep it down. My father will hear you.
DANNY. Fuck 'em.
ROBERTA. You got the most beautiful eyes.
DANNY. Shut up.
ROBERTA. I mean it.
DANNY. Shut up.
ROBERTA. Are you blushin?
DANNY. Fuck no. What the fuck you think I am?
ROBERTA. You are!
DANNY. I wanna ask you somethin.
ROBERTA. What?
DANNY. Who . . . I mean, how old are you?
ROBERTA. I already told ya! And you have a good memory!
DANNY. Right, right. So how old's your kid?
ROBERTA. You're just tryin to change the subject.
DANNY. So what if I am? No, really. I wanna know How old is he?
ROBERTA. He's gonna be thirteen.
DANNY. Old.
ROBERTA. Yeah. He's got big hands and feet. He's gonna be a big guy. Now he's gonna be in high school . . .
DANNY. Wow, you're gonna have a kid in high school.
ROBERTA. Yeah, ain't that a laugh? I hope he does better than I did. But he won't.
DANNY. Why not?
ROBERTA. He's all fucked up.
DANNY. What's wrong with him?
ROBERTA. He's a jerk. He's got me for a mother.
DANNY. It ain't his fault. (*She slaps him, suddenly furious.*)
ROBERTA. You're gonna be a wiseass why don't you just get the fuck outta here! I don't need that! I don't need anything like that!
DANNY. What's the fuck's with you?
ROBERTA. Sayin shit about the way I raise my kid!
DANNY. I didn't say nothin! You said it. And keep your hands to yourself or you could lose 'em!

ROBERTA. That kid was just born crazy, that's all. My mother don't understand that. Anyway, if anybody got him nuts it was her. All the time with the eyes. All the time not lookin at anybody . . .
DANNY. HEY! I never said nothin about your motherhood. You're probably good.
ROBERTA. No, I'm not.
DANNY. You probably are though.
ROBERTA. You think so?
DANNY. Sure.
ROBERTA. Thanks.
DANNY. You got some smack.
ROBERTA. You all right?
DANNY. No big deal. It almost felt . . . I feel good.
ROBERTA. So do I.
DANNY. It does look like the moon.
ROBERTA. You think so?
DANNY. Yeah. I was out in the country once. At night you never seen so many stars. It gave me a fuckin headache. Really. But then I saw there was this one bunch that looked like a big fish. A tuna or some shit. A big fish jumpin around in the stars. And cause I could see something in there, you know, somethin that added up, the whole thing didn't gimme a headache no more. That sound stupid?
ROBERTA. You must like the country.
DANNY. I hate the fuckin country.
ROBERTA. Why?
DANNY. All those fuckin trees. They smell bad.
ROBERTA. No!
DANNY. Yeah. They stink up everything out there like after-shave. And bugs all over the place. Mud. Rocks in your shoes. You can keep it.
ROBERTA. You're funny.
DANNY. Who's laughin?
ROBERTA. Not me.
DANNY. I had this teacher. He said I was stupid. Right in front of everybody. So I punched him in his fuckin eye. It swelled up real good. So they sent me to this camp in the woods to straighten my young ass out. I don't know what they was thinkin about. Gettin bit by a buncha bugs and sloppin through

the fuckin mud whadn't about to change my mind about some asshole teacher in James Monroe High School.
ROBERTA. I went to the deli this mornin to get a roll. Chinese guy put it in the bag. I looked at his face. And he was happy, I could tell. Bad things happen, I guess, to him sometimes, but you could see things whadn't bad for him.
DANNY. Let's go throw a rock through his window.
ROBERTA. No. I got another idea. Let's be like him, Danny. For tonight anyway. Let's be happy.
DANNY. Whaddaya talkin about?
ROBERTA. Let's be romantic.
DANNY. What?
ROBERTA. Let's be romantic with each other! Say things to each other!
DANNY. No. Like what?
ROBERTA. I don't know. Like . . . If you love me, I'll love you, too.
DANNY. I can't say shit like that.
ROBERTA. Sure you can! Oh, I don't know. Sure I do! Let's be romantic to each other, Danny! We've got a bed and we've . . . done love, and there's a candle and some kinda moon . . . What do we got? What do we got? Touch me. Put your hand on me nice and talk to me. (*Danny, with difficulty, touches her.*)
DANNY. You're a nut, huh?
ROBERTA. Nice?
DANNY. You're a . . . You . . . You're . . . good-lookin.
ROBERTA. No I'm not.
DANNY. Don't contradict me when I'm tellin you somethin!
ROBERTA. I'm sorry.
DANNY. You're good-lookin.
ROBERTA. Okay.
DANNY. (*Pause. He's working hard.*) You got a nice nose.
ROBERTA. A nice nose?
DANNY. Yeah. It's like . . . It looks at ya. That's right! It looks right at ya, your nose, and it says Hello! That's right! And you got a nice chin, too. When you, when you smile, it goes up. Yeah. Like a balloon. No. Better. Like a bird. Like some kinda bird.
ROBERTA. Thank you.
DANNY. Shut up! I ain't finished yet!

ROBERTA. You're not?
DANNY. No. What are you kiddin? I gotta tell you about your mouth. It's . . . It's . . . beautiful. Like a flower. That's right! A bird flyin and a flower, right there on your face. And all the time your nose sayin Hello.
ROBERTA. Stop!
DANNY. You know what?
ROBERTA. What?
DANNY. Say your name!
ROBERTA. Why?
DANNY. Just say it!
ROBERTA. Stop. Roberta.
DANNY. Say it again!
ROBERTA. Stop. Why?
DANNY. I wanna watch your mouth say your name. Say it again!
ROBERTA. Roberta.
DANNY. Again.
ROBERTA. Roberta. What are you doin?
DANNY. Watchin your beautiful mouth say your beautiful name.
ROBERTA. That's nice! You're bein so nice to me!
DANNY. Roberta.
ROBERTA. Stop!
DANNY. Why?
ROBERTA. It's like . . . tickling me.
DANNY. All right.
ROBERTA. Now I'll be nice to you!
DANNY. Nah.
ROBERTA. Yes, I will.
DANNY. You don't have to.
ROBERTA. Yes, I do too. I'll save your eyes for last. You did so good, I don't know what to say.
DANNY. Don't do nothin.
ROBERTA. Your hair! Your hair is very sexy.
DANNY. Shut up.
ROBERTA. Very sexy. Cause it's like strong and soft at the same time, and it feels good when you touch it.
DANNY. Comon, comon, let's talk about somethin else.
ROBERTA. All right. You got friendly ears.

DANNY. I ain't got friendly anything.
ROBERTA. You got friendly ears. They make me feel friendly.
They make me feel like, I wanna shake hands.
DANNY. This is so fuckin silly.
ROBERTA. Don't . . . curse.
DANNY. Okay.
ROBERTA. I was savin your eyes. Cause your eyes are very
dark and beautiful. And I don't think I know how to say things
about 'em. Your heart. I can see your heart. (*She leans forward to
kiss him, very slowly. As their lips are about to meet, in a panic, he slaps
her.*)
DANNY. No!
ROBERTA. (*Unshaken.*) Don't be scared, baby. (*This time she
succeeds in kissing him, first on his lips, then on each of his bruises.*)
DANNY. (*Weakly.*) No, no. Don't touch me. It burns.
ROBERTA. Somebody hurt my baby. Somebody hurt him.
Somebody hurt his hands. Somebody hurt his face. I love you,
Danny. I love you. I know you hurt, baby. I love you.
DANNY. What you doin to me?
ROBERTA. (*Kissing him.*) I'm lovin you.
DANNY. Stop.
ROBERTA. No.
DANNY. It's too much.
ROBERTA. Come on.
DANNY. I'm breathin.
ROBERTA. No you're not.
DANNY. I'm breathin too much.
ROBERTA. Don't worry about it.
DANNY. I'm gonna die from this.
ROBERTA. It's just an idea in your mind. Look at me. Look
at me. (*He looks at her.*)
DANNY. I . . . I . . . You're good . . . to be with.
ROBERTA. Oh, thank you, baby! Thank you! (*He slaps her.*)
DANNY. No! I can't . . . (*She goes right on kissing him.*)
ROBERTA. You don't have to be scared. You don't have to be.
I'm not gonna hurt you. I'm never gonna hurt you. (*He chokes
back a sob.*)
DANNY. I'm the Beast!
ROBERTA. No you're not. No you're not.
DANNY. Why you doin this for?

ROBERTA. I'm not doin nothin you ain't doin, too.
DANNY. Yeah?
ROBERTA. That's right. Do you really think you killed that guy?
DANNY. I don't know.
ROBERTA. I hope not.
DANNY. He was a real mess.
ROBERTA. But it takes a lot to kill somebody, right? I mean lots of people've been hurt worse than you hurt that guy, I bet, and they didn't die. Sure! That's right. Babies fall outta windows five stories high and go right on cryin. Old ladies get run over by buses and pop right back up. You hear about it all the time.
DANNY. I don't know. He wasn't . . . He wasn't dead when I left.
ROBERTA. Then you probably didn't kill nobody at all.
DANNY. I coulda killed him. Even if I didn't. Ain't that the same?
ROBERTA. Between you and me, yeah. It's the same. One way or the other. (*A distant boat horn sounds.*) Listen! (*It sounds again, and then once more.*) There. You hear it?
DANNY. What is it?
ROBERTA. Big boats.
DANNY. Ain't no boats around here. There's no water.
ROBERTA. Yeah, there is. It's not a block over or like that, but the ocean's right out there. (*The horn sounds again.*) See? That's a big boat goin down some like river to the ocean.
DANNY. Whatever you say.
ROBERTA. That's what it is. There's boats right up by Westchester Square. What's that, twenty blocks? Look sometime, you'll see 'em. Not the real big ones, but big. Sea boats. I met a sailor in the bar one time. In the outfit, you know? I was all over him. But he turned out to be nothin—a pothead. He giggled a lot. It was too bad because . . . Well, it was too bad. When we got married, me and Billy, that was my husband, we smoked a ball of opium one night. It really knocked me out. I fell asleep like immediately. And I dreamed about the ocean. It was real blue. And there was the sun, and it was real yellow. And I was out there, right in the middle of the ocean, and I heard this noise. I turned around, and whaddaya think I

saw? Just about right next to me. A whale! A whale came shootin straight outta the water! A whale! Yeah! And he opened up his mouth and closed it while he was up there in the air. And people on the boat said, Look! The whales are jumpin! And no shit, these whales start jumpin outta the water all over the place. And I can see them! Through one a those round windows. Or right out in the open. Whales! Gushin outta the water, and the water gushin outta their heads, you know, spoutin! And then, after a while, they all stopped jumpin. It got quiet. Everybody went away. The water smoothed out. But I kept lookin at the ocean. So deep and blue. And different. It was different then. 'Cause I knew it had all them whales in it.
DANNY. What if you . . . Nah, I ain't gonna say that.
ROBERTA. What were ya gonna say?
DANNY. Somethin I'm not gonna say. (*Referring to the doll.*) Is that you?
ROBERTA. That? It's just a doll.
DANNY. Yeah, I know that. But is it supposed to be you?
ROBERTA. Yeah, I guess so. Shirley gave it to me. My friend. When I was gonna get married.
DANNY. It don't look like you.
ROBERTA. No kiddin.
DANNY. It don't have your nose.
ROBERTA. No?
DANNY. No. Did you get in the whole white outfit, you know, when you got married?
ROBERTA. Not really. We got married at City Hall. My mother was pissed. She's religious. But we wanted to get that part over with. I was showin. It woulda been stupid in white. It's an ugly room, though, when they marry you at City Hall. It's like school.
DANNY. Why you keep the doll?
ROBERTA. It ain't much to keep.
DANNY. It's pretty.
ROBERTA. You think so?
DANNY. Bein a bride. All in white and everything. Flowers. I was at a weddin once. They left through this garden. All these roses all around. I never seen so many roses. Bees buzzin. Lotsa other flowers, too. They came out. Everybody was throwin rice. Why do they do that?

ROBERTA. I don't know.
DANNY. And then the bride came out. The groom was nothin. He looked good. (*Picks up the doll gently.*) But it was the bride. Here comes the bride, here comes the bride. I was sittin on this stone bench, waitin for 'em to come out. When I saw the bride, I stood up. She was so . . . I stood up. This big white dress. A veil. Flowers in her hand with ribbons blowin around. Little ribbons. And all around her. All these roses. And the bees buzzin. And nice girls. And everybody dressed in good clothes. Then everybody started throwin rice. Not hard. Nice and easy. Friendly. I forgot to throw mine. You wanna hear somethin really crazy? I mean, nuts?
ROBERTA. What?
DANNY. I'm not gonna tell ya.
ROBERTA. Comon, what?
DANNY. All right. I wanted to be the bride.
ROBERTA. That is nuts.
DANNY. I wanted to be the bride. Walkin out the big doors. All dressed in white. Music. Flowers all around. Everybody bein nice. Special, you know? Special. Yeah, I wanted to be the bride. (*Kisses the doll and places it gently back on the little shelf.*)
ROBERTA. Me too.
DANNY. You wanna marry me?
ROBERTA. Don't kid around.
DANNY. I'm serious.
ROBERTA. Stop it.
DANNY. Square business. You wanna marry me?
ROBERTA. No. Now let's talk about somethin else.
DANNY. Inna church? I wanna get married in that church with the garden. The one I was at.
ROBERTA. I told ya, don't kid around! Please!
DANNY. I ain't kiddin! I want you . . . to be a bride . . . with me.
ROBERTA. I got a kid.
DANNY. Let your parents take care of the kid.
ROBERTA. My parents.
DANNY. That's right! They fucked up your last marriage and they owe you somethin! Well comon, collect!
ROBERTA. I can't.
DANNY. Roberta. You got the right to somethin. Hey. Say your name for me.

ROBERTA. Roberta.
DANNY. Yeah. Roberta. That's you. And who am I?
ROBERTA. Danny.
DANNY. That's right. That's me. Will you marry me?
ROBERTA. All right. I mean, yes.
DANNY. You will?
ROBERTA. Yeah. I mean, yes.
DANNY. No! Yeah?
ROBERTA. Yeah!
DANNY. All right! Good! That's good! I feel like I won a prize or somethin.
ROBERTA. And will I wear a white dress?
DANNY. Yeah! Sure you will!
ROBERTA. And you'll wear the bow tie and everything?
DANNY. Yeah, yeah. The whole outfit.
ROBERTA. You think we could?
DANNY. Why not? People get married like that left and right!
ROBERTA. And we can go through the garden with all the flowers.
DANNY. That's right. I wanna go through the garden.
ROBERTA. And people will be throwin rice.
DANNY. Yeah, nice an easy. Underhand.
ROBERTA. And music. No guitars or anythin like that. An organ. A church organ.
DANNY. Okay.
ROBERTA. And we won't invite my father. We won't invite anybody we know. Maybe Shirley. No, not even Shirley. Just people we don't know. Nice people who go to weddings and throw rice.
DANNY. I gotta invite my mother.
ROBERTA. That's okay. I don't know her.
DANNY. And she could probably get us the cake. You know, cause she works in a bakery.
ROBERTA. A weddin cake. With the little you an the little me standin on top. An that thing around us.
DANNY. That's right.
ROBERTA. Where will we live?
DANNY. We'll get a place. Maybe out by Zerega. There's some nice places out by Zerega.
ROBERTA. Can I decorate it?
DANNY. Sure! Who else?

ROBERTA. I don't want anything Mediterranean. My mother's got all Mediterranean stuff.
DANNY. Okay. No Mediterranean.
ROBERTA. I like American furniture, you know? Maple. Shirley's got a maple chest a drawers. It's real nice. And solid! You could kick it and you'd just break your foot.
DANNY. I've been havin a lotta trouble on my job, you know? Cause I . . . Not a lotta trouble, you know, just some. Cause I fight a lot. The other guys play rugby, an they think I don't know nothin cause I don't know nothin about it. But I wouldn't have anymore trouble, you know, if I was married, you know? Settled down. And I pull down pretty good money, too. I ain't got nothin in the bank cause I never had no reason to save anything, you know? No reason to put nothin by. But we could save some money. It wouldn't take long. Buy some stuff. Lamps.
ROBERTA. And no kids!
DANNY. No?
ROBERTA. No.
DANNY. I thought I might like a kid.
ROBERTA. I don't want any.
DANNY. All right.
ROBERTA. Kids take all the money and you can't go nowhere. And if they get crazy or they're born crazy, everybody blames you, and they're around your neck like a rock on a chain. Just you and me, okay? Is that good with you?
DANNY. You got it. Gimme your hand. You're with me now. Everythin I make, you get half. Everything I feel, I'm gonna tell you. When I walk down the street, you'll be walkin with me.
ROBERTA. All right.
DANNY. Maybe, like on Sunday, we can go to Hampton House. Have breakfast. They gotta special breakfast. People go there.
ROBERTA. We're gonna haveta announce the weddin.
DANNY. Yeah?
ROBERTA. Yeah. You gotta have an announcement for a church weddin. Banns.
DANNY. Oh yeah, right. So we'll do that.
ROBERTA. Ah no, we can't get married inna church, though.
DANNY. Why not?

ROBERTA. I'm divorced.
DANNY. So?
ROBERTA. They won't let ya.
DANNY. We won't tell 'em.
ROBERTA. They'll find out.
DANNY. No, they won't.
ROBERTA. There's papers you gotta do an stuff. They'd know.
DANNY. Hey, my mother's Protestant. We'll get married Protestant.
ROBERTA. They don't care?
DANNY. No. You can be divorced.
ROBERTA. Really? I guess that's right.
DANNY. It don't make no difference to Protestants.
ROBERTA. And are their churches like, real?
DANNY. Yeah. They're great!
ROBERTA. And I can still wear the white an everything?
DANNY. Yeah, sure.
ROBERTA. My parents'd go through the roof if I got married Protestant. I bet my mother'd go off her nut.
DANNY. They're not invited, remember?
ROBERTA. That's right.
DANNY. Fuck 'em.
ROBERTA. Yeah.
DANNY. You're with me now.
ROBERTA. Okay.
DANNY. The moon just went out.
ROBERTA. He's got it on a timer.
DANNY. It's almost the mornin.
ROBERTA. Seems like it couldn't be.
DANNY. Why not?
ROBERTA. Too quick.
DANNY. Yeah.
ROBERTA. I'm glad. I'm glad.
DANNY. You tired?
ROBERTA. Yeah. I'm gonna sleep. You sleep, too.
DANNY. Yeah. (*She turns out the little lamp. Just the candle burns. Only Danny is visible.*)
ROBERTA. Kiss me. (*He does.*) Thank you.
DANNY. You're welcome.

ROBERTA. You talked to me nice, Danny. Romantic. I can never get to sleep good. Couldn't close my eyes, you know? Cause if I closed my eyes, I was just in my head. And I couldn't hack it. In my head. Buildin's burnin and people fallin in cracks in the ground. My father. My kid. My mother prayin. Rainin floods. You never know whether it's a puddle or you step in the wrong spot and you drown. But this is real good. My head's shuttin down. All I can see in here's the moon, floatin over everything quiet. Like a bride. All dressed in white. I can smell the roses. Can you?
DANNY. Yeah.
ROBERTA. An the bees are hummin. (*She hums "Here Comes The Bride" softly and falls asleep.*)
DANNY. It's good. It's good. Hey, I didn't know that about what you told me, the ocean bein right here. Think a that. Maybe that's what we oughta do. Build a boat and sail the fuck away. Get married on some island where everybody speaks Booga Booga. Are you asleep? I love you. (*Danny blows out the candle. The first hint of dawn is in the window. A bird gently sings the first notes of a morning song. The lights go down.*)

SCENE 3

Lights up. The bedroom. It's late morning. Roberta and Danny are asleep. Danny is snoring. Roberta wakes up. She touches Danny's face tenderly, then hits him with a pillow.

ROBERTA. Tag!
DANNY. (*Snapping into a violent stance.*) What?!
ROBERTA. You're it. Good mornin!
DANNY. Oh yeah. Good mornin.
ROBERTA. Keep it down a bit.
DANNY. Why?
ROBERTA. My family.
DANNY. Oh. Okay.
ROBERTA. They'll be gone inna minute. Then I'll cook you breakfast if you want.
DANNY. Sure. Where they goin?
ROBERTA. The kid goes to school. At least he leaves here

with books. My mother goes to work. My father goes to work.
DANNY. What about you?
ROBERTA. I don't work. Not right now. I didn't like my last
job so I quit.
DANNY. What did you do?
ROBERTA. I was a secretary for a bunch a exterminators.
DANNY. You're kiddin?
ROBERTA. Nope. They had this truck with a big dead roach
on top, an they were real nasty to me, and at night, I used to
dream the truck was chasin me an the roach was movin. So I
quit. I gotta get somethin else, but I ain't started lookin yet.
What about your job? When you gotta be there?
DANNY. They don't need me till Wednesday this week. It's a
slow time.
ROBERTA. So how do I look in the daylight?
DANNY. Good.
ROBERTA. You still like my nose?
DANNY. Oh yeah.
ROBERTA. You don't have to, you know.
DANNY. Whaddaya mean?
ROBERTA. You know.
DANNY. No, I don't.
ROBERTA. You don't haveta stick to nothin you said last
night. It was nice that you said it at all. I slept good last night
for about the first time inna fuckin century.
DANNY. Whaddaya think I am?
ROBERTA. I think you're real nice. An I like ya. That's why
I'm sayin what I'm sayin. So you won't haveta. You like eggs for
breakfast? I think there'll be some.
DANNY. I meant last night. What I said.
ROBERTA. You don't haveta say that.
DANNY. I did!
ROBERTA. Aw comon, Danny.
DANNY. I asked ya ta marry me last night square business an
you said yes an I meant it!
ROBERTA. All right then, I didn't!
DANNY. What?
ROBERTA. You heard me!
DANNY. What?
ROBERTA. I was lyin cause I wanted a nice thing. Get

serious. No way are you an me gettin married. That was strictly make-believe.
DANNY. Don't do this to me!
ROBERTA. I gotta kid, a fucked up kid, no job, crazy parents. I'm crazy myself. I told you. Last night. Wake up. Open your fuckin eyes. I ain't got no serious way possible I could get married to anybody. Not anybody. No less a guy like you.
DANNY. Whaddaya mean, a guy like me?
ROBERTA. Nothin, all right?
DANNY. Tell me what you mean!
ROBERTA. You know.
DANNY. I don't know nothin!
ROBERTA. Look at your hands, Danny. Why do you wanna make me say it? You're all fucked up. If ya didn't kill somebody the other night, ya will sometime. If I married ya, it could be me. Yud haveta be retarded not to see it! You're a fuckin caveman! Yud be bouncin me off the walls . . .
DANNY. NO!
ROBERTA. You grabbed me last night. See the mark?
DANNY. I'm sorry I hurt your throat.
ROBERTA. I'll make you breakfast. Then you'll go back to Zerega.
DANNY. No.
ROBERTA. Then you'll go wherever, but you'll go.
DANNY. I don't buy this line a shit, Roberta. Not just cause it makes me feel bad. It don't sound true to me.
ROBERTA. It don't matter how it sounds.
DANNY. Yeah, it matters! I heard the way you really are last night. It whadn't this. Ya wanted to show somebody how ya really was last night. Ya showed me.
ROBERTA. This is how I really am! Last night was just time out.
DANNY. You're lyin!
ROBERTA. And you're still dreamin!
DANNY. No I'm not.
ROBERTA. I don't wanna talk. I don't care.
DANNY. I care. I gotta care.
ROBERTA. Well don't bother me with it.
DANNY. You gotta be straight with me at least.
ROBERTA. I don't gotta do nothin.

DANNY. You do too! You were gonna marry me last night.
ROBERTA. I can't marry ya!
DANNY. Tell me why!
ROBERTA. I told ya!
DANNY. I know I'm fucked up! But I got control! Don't do this to me, Roberta! Ya kissed my hands. Ya kissed my hands. It ain't right ta do this to me. I got a heart in my body and it's gonna break and it's gonna be you that did it. What can I tell you? What can I tell you that'll make you like you were to me?
ROBERTA. Danny.
DANNY. Anything. Don't just . . . just don't say no.
ROBERTA. I can't, baby. I can't.
DANNY. Why not?
ROBERTA. Just leave it.
DANNY. I can't go back.
ROBERTA. I heard the bird sing that sings outside my window. This mornin. When I was just gone asleep. I heard ya talkin an the bird singin. An it was the first time I could sleep right . . . since I was a young girl. But I'm sorry I told ya yes, cause I can't marry ya, baby. Just take it outta ya mind. It wouldn't be right.
DANNY. There's a way ta make it right, if ya know enough! Tell me what's the matter an we'll make it right! There's people we can go to if we don't know enough between us. There's people an a way if ya want it bad enough, but ya just don't know how. An I want it bad an I think you do too! Do ya wanna marry me, Roberta?
ROBERTA. Sure. I mean no. I mean I can't.
DANNY. What's the thing?
ROBERTA. Nothin.
DANNY. What's the thing?
ROBERTA. I told ya.
DANNY. Told me what?
ROBERTA. About my father.
DANNY. So ya told me.
ROBERTA. Ya can't do a horrible thing like that, Danny, an not be punished. It was me that did it.
DANNY. Whaddaya talkin about?
ROBERTA. I did a bad thing.
DANNY. All right! So ya did a bad thing. Ya told me.

ROBERTA. An . . . An . . . nobody punished me.
DANNY. Good.
ROBERTA. No! No, it ain't good! I did a bad thing an nobody
punished me, and so . . . it stayed with me.
DANNY. I don't get you.
ROBERTA. I made my father inta garbage. I made myself
that way, too. It's all wrong. My mother don't know what happened, but she knows. Cause it stinks so bad. I can hear her
prayin all the time. Crazy whinin prayin like needles. An when
she's not prayin, she's lookin around like she lost somethin but
she ain't lookin for anythin an SHE WON'T LOOK AT ME!
At the floor the wall anythin but not me! An my kid. I did that
an I got a kid. I had no right to do what I did! It was too bad a
thing to do. There's no happy thing possible becausa me. It's
my house. It's my garbage. I can't leave this house cause it's my
crime.
DANNY. That's crazy.
ROBERTA. So what? Just cause it's crazy don't mean it ain't
true.
DANNY. You can do whatever you want.
ROBERTA. I did whatever I wanted, an it killed my whole
fuckin family! I don't mean ta spill my poison any further than I
already have! Ya hear me? It's over. I'm through screwin
everythin up. I went out last night cause I couldn't stand it in
this room anymore. I couldn't stand bein by myself anymore,
with myself anymore. I talked ta you cause I hadda talk to
somebody, somebody, an there you were, so fucked up ya
might listen.
DANNY. Roberta . . .
ROBERTA. No. An ya did listen. An I thank ya for it. An I
slept last night so sweet, for the first time inna hundred years.
Cause you were good ta me an talked nice. But that's it, man.
That is strictly fuckin it. Cause this is my house. My house.
And I gotta live in it.
DANNY. I'm takin you outta here.
ROBERTA. Forget it. It ain't gonna happen.
DANNY. I have to!
ROBERTA. You can't!
DANNY. I love you.
ROBERTA. You just need ta say that for your own private

fuckin reasons! You don't know me. It ain't possible ta know somebody that fuckin quick. I told ya last night, an I'm telling you now. I'm nuts! An I'll tell you what I didn't tell you then. I'm bad.

DANNY. Oh comon, gimme a break.

ROBERTA. I gotta badness in me. I did what I did ta my father an my family cause there's a big mean bad feelin in me that like ta break an hurt, and I'd break and hurt you just the same. Just the same as I did them.

DANNY. Get serious. You would not.

ROBERTA. You ain't nothin ta me! You ain't dog shit on my shoes! Get outta here, freak! With yar crazy fights. Go back to the cave ya crawled out of! Go beat up a wall! Go watch yar dishrag mother puke her dishrag guts! Ya fuckin Beast! Ya fuckin Beast! Ya got to screw the pig, and if ya'd played yar cards right, ya mighta got a free breakfast! But ya blew it, so get the fuck out! Get out! Get out! Get out, ya moron clown! Get the fuck outta here an leave me, leave me alone! (*She collapses, sobbing. Quiets.*)

DANNY. I ain't too good at people. But I gotta say somethin. A crazy thing. To you. An you gotta let me say it. (*Embarassed.*) I . . . forgive you.

ROBERTA. What?

DANNY. I forgive you. Everythin you done.

ROBERTA. You can't do that.

DANNY. I gotta be able. You gotta let me be.

ROBERTA. I can't.

DANNY. You gotta let go. Let go of it.

ROBERTA. You don't know what you're sayin.

DANNY. I know. You told me . . . what you done. An I don't care. There ain't nobody else. An it's gotta happen. So I do it. I forgive you. You're forgiven.

ROBERTA. Whaddaya think you are, a priest?

DANNY. I am whatever I gotta be. It's over now. You've felt bad long enough. You did a bad thing. An it's been bitin you in the head for a long time. It's a long enough time. You paid for what you done. That's why you got me last night. That's why you brought me here. You knew . . . you'd paid up. That's why you told me your bad thing.

ROBERTA. You can't forgive me.

DANNY. Yes, I can.

ROBERTA. No! (*He pulls her to him, and over his knee. He spanks her.*)

DANNY. That's for doin what you did. All right? That's the punishment.

ROBERTA. I'm sorry. I didn't mean it. It just happened. It was . . . I'm sorry, I'm sorry, I'm sorry. Please . . .

DANNY. (*Putting a hand on her.*) I forgive you. It's done. I've done it. It's done.

ROBERTA. Yeah?

DANNY. Yeah.

ROBERTA. Thank you.

DANNY. You're welcome.

ROBERTA. Thank you.

DANNY. We were bullshit last night. It was bullshit. I'm not too good. At tellin the difference. I ain't been too good at people. Ever. But what we were makin believe, other people got.

ROBERTA. That's other people.

DANNY. But if we want, why can't we?

ROBERTA. I don't know.

DANNY. It ain't a lot, what I want. I don't see why I can't get it. I know there ain't no way my whole life's gonna turn a corner an be the perfect thing. Yours neither. But I can get a day, can't I? To start with? That seems like somethin I could get.

ROBERTA. What day?

DANNY. Weddin day.

ROBERTA. No . . .

DANNY. Listen. We could have a weddin day. You be dressed in white. The flowers. Everythin we said. Pretty much. I gotta job. I'll get the money. If you get a job, that's good, too. We'll plan it out. There don't haveta be no hurry with it. It'd be somethin ta make happen.

ROBERTA. It don't make no sense ta do it.

DANNY. Just cause it don't make no sense don't mean it ain't true. It could be true. If you want it. I ain't never planned no single fuckin thing in my life. I ain't never done nothin. Things happen to me. Me, you, what you did. We didn't do that stuff. It happened ta us. That's why you're sayin no, Roberta. It's cause ya think we can't do nothin. Like it's always been, right? But we

can. We can plan a weddin, an the weddin'ill happen the way
we plan. The only surprise will be that we knew.
ROBERTA. Yeah? You think so?
DANNY. Yeah. I do. I definitely definitely think I do. (*The
lights fade.*)

THE END

PROPERTY LIST

Scene One

Bowl of pretzels
Pitcher of beer
Glasses (2)
Small tables (2)
Chairs (2)

Scene Two

Mattress
Lamp
Stool
Shelves
Doll, dressed as a bride, on shelf
Candle
Wine bottle
Metal cup